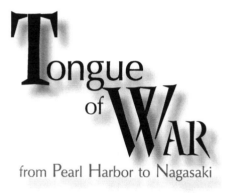

Tongue of WAR

from Pearl Harbor to Nagasaki

Tony Barnstone

winner of the John Ciardi Prize for Poetry
selected by B. H. Fairchild

BkMk Press
University of Missouri-Kansas City

BkMk Press
University of Missouri-Kansas City
5101 Rockhill Road
Kansas City, Missouri 64110
(816) 235-2558 (voice)
(816) 235-2611 (fax)
www.umkc.edu/bkmk

Cover art: David Zung
Author photo: Elli Tzalopoulou Barnstone
Book Design: Susan L. Schurman
Managing Editor: Ben Furnish
Associate Editor: Michelle Boisseau
Editorial Assistant: Elizabeth Gromling
BkMk Press wishes to thank Lindsey Martin-Bowen,
Susan Cobin, Greg Field, Steve Gehrke, Andrés Rodríguez,
Maryfrances Wagner, Karen I. Johnson, Joni Lee, and Destiny Vinley.

Previous winners of the John Ciardi Prize for Poetry: *Black Tupelo Country* by Doug Ramspeck, selected by Leslie Adrienne Miller; *Voices* by Paula Bonnell, selected by Mark Jarman; *Wayne's College of Beauty* by David Swanger, selected by Colleen J. McElroy; *The Portable Famine* by Rane Arroyo, selected by Robin Becker; *Fence Line* by Curtis Bauer, selected by Christopher Buckley; *Escape Artist* by Terry Blackhawk, selected by Molly Peacock; *Kentucky Swami* by Tim Skeen, selected by Michael Burns; *The Resurrection Machine* by Steve Gehrke, selected by Miller Williams.

Library of Congress Cataloging-in-Publication Data

Barnstone, Tony.
  Tongue of war : from Pearl Harbor to Nagasaki: poems / Tony Barnstone
      p. cm.
  "Winner of the John Ciardi Prize for Poetry selected by B.H. Fairchild."
  Summary: "These poems, many written in forms such as the sonnet, are
inspired by historical situations and accounts--letters, oral histories, news
reports, etc.--of individuals from both sides of the Pacific theater of World War
II, including the home fronts"--Provided by publisher.
  ISBN 978-1-886157-71-2 (pbk. : alk. paper)
  1. World War, 1939-1945--Poetry. I. Title. II. Title: Pearl Harbor to Nagasaki:
poems.
  PS3552.A7215T66 2009
  811'.54--dc22

                        2009039470

This book is set in Nyx, Optima, and Bodoni SvtyTwo ITC typefaces

Acknowledgments

Thanks to the National Endowment for the Arts and to the California Arts Council for fellowships that supported me during the writing of this book. "White Fear" won the Strokestown International Poetry Award, 2008 (grand prize). Thanks also to B.H. Fairchild for choosing this volume for the John Ciardi Prize in Poetry. I am particularly happy to receive an award named for Ciardi, who flew twenty missions over Japan in World War II as a gunner on B-29 airplanes, and whose poetry and memoir, *Saipan*, are important literary texts about the war in the Pacific. Thanks to Willis Barnstone, Sholeh Wolpe, Alan Michael Parker, Michelle Boisseau, and Caroline Heldman for their support for this project and their comments on these poems. The poems listed below have appeared in the publications noted, sometimes in earlier versions.

TriQuarterly: "The Trinity Test," "Holocausts of Water and Fire," "The Pilot's Tale," "Milk Run," "Rosie the Riveter," "The Pit," "The Man Who Won the War"

Kyoto Journal: "The Trinity Test," "Holocausts of Water and Fire," "Fireflies Over Tokyo," "The Bombardier's Tale"

Michigan Quarterly Review: "Forced March"

66: Sonnet Studies: "Angel of Death," "The Burma Road," "On the Day Japan Surrenders"

Locus Point: "The Battle for Saipan," "The Power of a God," "The Thin Man"

Margie: "Wartime Medicine," "Home Brew"

In the Black/In the Red: Poems of Profit & Loss, edited by Gloria Vando and Philip Miller (Helicon Nine Editions): "Seeds of Gold"

Prairie Margins: "Seeds of Gold," "The Cannibals"

Born Magazine (www.bornmagazine.com): "Hospital Tent" (multimedia collaboration with artists Jonathan Minori and Fabrizio Aiello)

Poetry International: "Nagasaki Drop," "Mass Suicide, Okinawa," "A Farewell to Arms"

Court Green: "Camp Morale," "Disappearing Act"

The Drunken Boat: "Roast Fish and Sweet Yams," "White Bones," "Chopsticks," "Snapshot," "Morning in Hiroshima," "The School-girl's Tale"

Runes (Storm Issue): "A Black Rain Fell"

Measure: "Revenant," "War Sickness," "Not Enough," "Survivor," "Grace Under Pressure"

The Comstock Review: "The Birds of Pearl Harbor," "Beach Landing, Iwo Jima"

The Cortland Review: "The Cave," "White Pig, Dark Pig," "Reversal at the Battle of Midway," "The Forge"

Jacket: "The Cannibals"

Spillway: "I'm Used to It," "Jacob's Ladder," "The Bataan Death March," "Horse Cock and Cheese"

Poetry Ireland: "White Fear"

Pif Magazine: "Benito Mussolini," "Massacre Bay," "The Ball Turret Gunner"

For my mother, Elli Tzalopoulou Barnstone,
and my father, Willis Barnstone

Tongue of WAR

BEGINNINGS

THE ISLAND CAMPAIGN

THE BOMB

ENDINGS

So listen folks, for here's my thesis,
Peace in the world, or the world in pieces.
—1947 country-western song

I know not with what weapons World War III will be fought, but World War IV will be fought with sticks and stones.
—Albert Einstein

Foreword

Tongue of War is one of the most distinctive poetry manuscripts I have ever judged for a book prize. (And it is a book rather than simply a collection.) Everything about it cuts against the current fashions. It is about war—in particular the war in the Pacific which continues to haunt post-1945 American and Japanese cultures, the war from which many older men and women still have not returned ("There is the man in the war and, later, the war in the man.") It is written in forms, especially the sonnet, and of course the meter of those forms, the pulse of human feeling unable to name itself, belying once again the notion that the music of poetry somehow distorts rather than embodies and intensifies the real stuff of human experience. The diction and syntax are often blunt with the exhaustion and terror of human voices—American and Japanese, soldiers and civilians—struggling to articulate the unspeakable, to make visible that to which we have learned to blind ourselves. The voices are as various—guilt-ridden, cynical, stunned, meditative, angry, indifferent, traumatized, proud, regretful—as the nearly infinite shades of the war experience itself. Such is the power of Tongue of War that I cannot help but think that having read it, an American President who has himself been privileged to avoid the horrors of the battlefield might be less inclined to send young men and women off to face them.

—B.H. Fairchild

Introduction

Tongue of War originated on November 1st, 1995 with an invitation to have dinner with Brigadier General Paul Tibbets (1915-2007), pilot of the Enola Gay. It was an invitation I had deep reservations about, not least because my then-wife and in-laws were Japanese-American. Nonetheless, pulled by a sense of morbid curiosity, a need to look in the face of history, I went.

At our strange dinner, I asked him what his response was to recent revisionist histories that have questioned the morality of the decision to drop the bomb on Hiroshima. A pugnacious, white-haired fellow with protruding ears, he looked harmless, like one of the seven dwarfs, but he was a forceful presence, clearheaded, with a powerful memory, and his reply was fierce: "You can't rewrite history....If people today could only see the attitude we had, the patriotism, and the sincerity of our beliefs." General Tibbets was the one man I knew who really believed in the bomb. Perhaps he had to. He was a patriot with not an ounce of doubt that he did the right thing. He believed in the story of the army: honor, duty, following orders, necessary violence. And he believed in the official story of the bomb—that he was a hero who saved a million lives, that the bomb had to be dropped on a city, not on a demonstration site, and that those who were killed got what they deserved.

When asked if he had any qualms about dropping such a devastating weapon on a civilian population, he said something that still eats at me: "All people were fair game....There is no such thing as separating the innocent from the guilty, because everyone is guilty. The days of knights meeting out on a field and fighting one to one is over for a long time now." The first poem I wrote in the Tongue of War sequence was a sonnet constructed as a dramatic monologue building upon the General's public statements about his feelings about dropping the bomb.

From this start, I branched out and spent a decade and a half researching war letters, diaries, histories, oral histories, and interviews with American and Japanese soldiers, scientists such as Robert Oppenheimer, President Harry Truman, and citizen survivors of the Rape of Nanjing, of Hiroshima, and of Nagasaki. Drawing from these sources, these poems speak from the points of view of participants in, observers of, and victims of the war. I know that it is out of fashion to speak of morality in poetry, but I see this sequence as having a serious moral basis. It is an attempt to create not a simplistic story with a single moral at the end, but a story that brings alive the experiences of the individual participants in all their variety, limitations, and complications—showing their anger, their mutual racial hatred and fear, their suffering, and their attempts to make peace with events of unspeakable horror.

I see the sequence as a history in verse in which I allow the readers to inhabit multiple and warring perspectives on key events of the War in the Pacific (the attack on Pearl Harbor, the internment of Japanese Americans, war crimes such as torture, cannibalism and medical experiments on live prisoners, the firebombing of Tokyo and the bombing of Hiroshima and Nagasaki) so as to draw their own conclusions. I wanted to allow the contradictions and complications of the moral questions here to remain contradictory and complicated, because as I delved into my research it became clear that each person who speaks in the sequence would respond to these events in a different way, and feel justified in his or her response. A radiation sickness victim on the ground who lost his or her home and family has a radically different perspective on the bombing of Hiroshima than an American soldier awaiting the final bloody invasion of the Japanese mainland.

The texts I consulted were so intrinsically powerful in and of themselves, so imbued with a radiation charge of the appalling as to need little narrative invention from me. Nevertheless, the sequence was extremely difficult to write. It was hellish to read of the effects of the atom bomb on the civilians on the ground, and just as difficult was the research I did into the firebombing of Tokyo, the horrific conditions in Japanese prisoner-of-war camps, the Bataan Death March, the live-subject medical research performed by Japanese doctors in China, and the beheading of captured American pilots. I could understand why Theodor Adorno observed that there could be no poetry after the Holocaust. Perhaps there could be no poetry after Hiroshima. I found these voices so personally devastating, so emotionally shocking as to leave me at times paralyzed before them. They were nitroglycerine; I was afraid to touch them. Yet the voices continued to clamor about what they had seen. In the end, I decided to remove myself from the process as much as possible, to approach the task as a kind of objective poetic journalism. I did my best to shut up and get out of the way and let the characters speak directly, in their own tone, diction and rhetoric.

I see this book as a love letter to the World War II generation. It is not a book that glosses over the war profiteering, the execution of prisoners, the torture, the massacres of civilians, the rape and the sex slavery, but rather one that seeks a broad understanding of the pressures and the perspectives of those who lived through this extraordinary period. The discourse of hero and villain elides our full humanity. According to Japanese esthetics, the object is of most interest before or after the climax (the flower bud, not its full bloom; the cracked teapot, not the perfect one), whereas in the West we tend to emphasize climax, epiphany, the world and the mind at its height. The man who was a hero at Iwo Jima was a scared teenager and a high school bully who came home and fought his memories and alcoholism. The villain who massacred civilians was beaten by his stepfather and spent years later trying to simultaneously hide from and atone for his past. Our lives are a moral continuum, not something to be judged by our best and worst moments.

Let me give you an example. One of the most moving oral histories I read was from the point of view of a Japanese war criminal, a man who in order to become an officer had to prove his worth by chopping off the head of a Chinese prisoner with his samurai sword in one fierce stroke. He did so, and in that moment, he says, he lost his humanity. He had learned the lesson well, and so as an officer he had his soldiers practice bayonet stabs on live prisoners, training them to be dead cold, unflinching killers like him.

At the end of the war, he was captured by the Chinese and imprisoned. While in prison, his Chinese captors asked him and his fellow prisoners to write confessions of their crimes. He promptly did so, and was the first in the room to march to the front with several pages of closely-written text. The Chinese officer immediately ripped up his confession, telling him he wrote it too quickly, so had clearly not reflected with his heart upon his crimes. He was put into solitary confinement in a prison cell underground, and while there he read on the wall characters written by Chinese prisoners who had been imprisoned by the Japanese, perhaps by him. He saw in the slogans on the wall such humanity, such pride, and such resistance to the Japanese invaders that he realized for the first time that he had been wrong in his disdain for the Chinese, wrong in considering them an inferior race. In that moment he broke down weeping and regained his humanity. Later, he was repatriated to Japan.

This is the sort of story I wish to tell in *Tongue of War*—the story of how historical pressures can make one into a monster or into a human being. It is the story of the War in the Pacific told from the worm's eye view, and it is a story that I hope will help my readers better understand our common humanity.

—Tony Barnstone

BEGINNINGS

Angel of Death

I showered, shaved and slid down to the mess
for breakfast, then at 0800 heard
a plane commence a dive. I watched that bird
till something dropped off it. Yeah, I confess.
I didn't get it. Just a mock air raid,
I thought. And then a water geyser shot
into the air three hundred feet. I got
it then. I saw red meatball wings, and said,
"Those are Jap planes, they're bombing us!" One plane
plunged toward me and I ran as concrete chips
kicked up around me. I ate dirt. The fighter
passed over me, angel of death. The flame
ate into Heaven from the burning ships,
but I had lived. The sky was never brighter.

Radioman, Ford Island, Pearl Harbor, 1941

Jacob's Ladder

From forward we were ordered aft, five decks
below, to send up ammunition from
the magazines. That job was on our necks.
The Arizona shuddered like a drum,
and with a roar the forward magazine
went nova, with one million pounds of powder.
Through sooty blackness I climbed, climbed through dream
with grappling hands, and almost dropped. But power
from some strange source filled me, and so I hung
onto the red-hot ladder, my head light,
smelling my own baked flesh, each searing rung
eating my hands, and climbed up to the light.
I climbed till I was out—out of my head
—then lay down on the deck among the dead.

Seaman, USS Arizona, Pearl Harbor, 1941

The Forge

And when I surfaced topside from the dark
the air was red as if the world were rusting.
The zeros swooped around us in a ring
of silver, smoke was blossoming, hot sparks
were skittering, fuel oil poured out on the water,
and like a metal pot stuck in the center
on a gas stove, we cooked. I'll tell you square,
I lost it, on my knees like at an altar,
till all the beaten metal made dream music.
I almost died, but smoke sharp in my nose,
heat on my face, woke me. Out of the clatter
inside my head I dove, swam from the rows
of ships, then turned and watched flames swell and flick.
I watched as that punk Death worked at the bellows.

Seaman, USS Arizona, Pearl Harbor, 1941

The Birds of Pearl Harbor

Like geese, they came at us in gaggles.
I saw one airplane coming in,
saw clear the pilot with dark goggles
and even thought I saw him grin
as he flew low through bursts of flak,
loosed his torpedoes at us like
finned dolphins, banked, then joined the flock.
The harbor was a flaming lake
of oil, with seamen swimming there
like angels dropped in yellow hell,
but I jumped in and swam. The air
was death to breathe and full of hail
from shrapnel so I swam through blue
until it seemed my head would bust.

I surfaced and looked back. A blow
shuddered the waters, a red blast,
and that was when the ship went up,
with God's own store of gunpowder,
end of the world. Why I get up
each day alive, what queer power
that wet and smoky oily dawn
spared me to go back to my wife,
to live here with a house and lawn,
I just don't know. Why give me life?
I guess that's what the ones who lived
all ask, strange men swatting at bees
in the park, ducking pigeons dive-
bombing our bread, kicking the geese.

Crewman, U.S.S. Arizona, Pearl Harbor, 1941

They Could Have Given It to Us

but they kept every drop of oil.
That's why the need to kill flared up
like hot gas in our blood and boiled
all Buddhist conscience out of us.
Today I am a priest, and still
I use the discipline I learned
at the Academy. To kill
is wrong. I know. But then I burned
for it. Pearl Harbor made me burst
with joy. We needed oil, just that.
We had no choice but to strike first.
A cornered mouse will bite a cat.

Japanese Naval Officer, Pearl Harbor, 1941

Disappearing Act

And then one day the streets were empty. And
then one day our neighbors all were gone.
Alkazam! Poof! A magic act. At gun-
point these Americans were taken: hand
over your house, your business, farm. They're not
yours anymore. Now grab what you can carry
and board the train. And like a cemetery
our town filled up with emptiness. At night
the vacant houses watched me, and in fright
I'd burst out singing "Pistol Packin' Mama"
and then I'd run past them, lickety-kite.
I had the normal tussles, childhood drama,
and called the kids I fought "Dirty Jap rat,"
and hid my German blood. Whites could do that.

Boy, Sioux Falls, South Dakota, 1942

Benito Mussolini

They didn't put us in the camps like Japs
but called us names like "Greasy guinea." See, we
were poor, my parents couldn't read, and perhaps
we should have been in camp since Mussolini
was a big deal to us, okay? At last
our Italy had someone who was not
a wimp. But how we felt on that changed fast
when we got in the war, when we was caught
up in the thing, and when the navy took
my boys and I lost one in the Pacific,
and I worked factory, one parachute
each minute. So I thought it was terrific
when Mussolini was arrested. Brute,
buffoon, they hung Il Duce from a hook.

Factory worker, Little Italy, New York

I'm Used to It

I'm used to it.
Once a man came up to me
and said, "Hello, Sonny boy!"
and then for no reason I could see
punched me in the temple
and walked off down the street.
He didn't even
call out "Go back home!"
or "Yellow dog!"
like the others did.
I wrote a poem about it:

> Even the purple welt
> on my head is more American
> than you are, Mister!

Now in the camp here's what I'm used to:
I sleep in dust and eat the dust,
they don't even let me bathe
and I am rotting, my hair growing
every which way. I chew off
my fingernails but have no way
to cut the nails on my toes.

> Am I a dog to you?
> But even dogs get bathed sometimes,
> you dirty guard. Woof!

They shot into a crowd of us
and killed a man.

That's hard to get used to.
Then they shot one of us
in the back. That night we wept
and pounded on the table.

A hole in his back.
Empty space at the table.
No one will sit there.

I hear the sister kept the tee-shirt
with a bloody hole in the back.
She held on to it for years
but her brother was dead
and no one cared.
Finally she buried the thing.

Prisoner, Japanese-American Internment Camp, 1942

Forced March

I was a scholar in Nanjing until
the Japanese took me. Smoke rises from
the broken houses by the road. I'm dumb
with grief, my legs are quaking, but I kill
some time by chanting poems beneath my breath.
White bones are tangled in the brush. The vase
of China has been shattered. Still, I chase
a hope or two. I'm not yet in the earth.
At dusk we fall down in the road, our hair
wild grass, our shirts torn clouds, and sleep. I shiver
through a deep dream, confused. Did someone scream,
or was it me? Was that a sob? I hear
the wind blow rain, as on an icy river
great iron horses gallop through my dream.

Professor, National Central University, Nanjing, 1937

Revenant

I knew the Chinese were inferiors,
a backward race, but still was shocked to see
them by the pit, lined up and bound for me
to kill. That's how they made us officers
hard as the steel blades used to lop off heads.
Headless, the corpses lost identity.
I, too, was cut off from humanity.
I killed myself that day, and lived on, dead.
I had my soldiers bayonet the men
we captured—prisoners were too much bother.
My men became like me, dead cold. And then
we burned the houses, raped the women. Other
men couldn't kill like that, were a disgrace,
but I would not be shamed. I saved my face.

Japanese Officer, Nanjing, 1937

Facing Nanjing

The men who couldn't kill were a disgrace,
but I would not be shamed. I saved my face.
Later, when we were captured by Chinese
troops and interrogated about these
events, I wrote a full confession, marched
up to the officer with several pages,
strangely proud to finish first. He arched
an eyebrow, then he tore my careful pages
into four pieces. "Fast," he said. "Too fast.
You need to *think* about your crimes." They tossed
me in a cell to think, a cell where men
were tortured by my troops. While dead months passed
I read graffiti written there in blood,
and understood. I faced it there: how lost
I was, how much I'd lost, and wept, a flood.
Tell me, how can I be a man again?

Japanese Officer, Nanjing, 1937

THE ISLAND CAMPAIGN

Hospital Tent

I looked around the scene, and saw the men,
some dead, some twisting on the tables, smell
of antiseptic, smell of blood, and then
I looked outside where more waited. I tell
you I knew nothing of the Philippines,
of mangoes, houses on stilts, nipa huts,
the smell of copra in the air, gangrene
and amputations, lice, the surgeon's cuts
I had to sew back up, of carabao,
the glisten of the small steel instruments
catching the glint of lantern light, red pile
of gauze. But still I never cried
until one day when (I did not see how)
my hand was grabbed as I passed by, intent,
by a young man who gave me half a smile
and held me with his hands and eyes—then died.

U.S. Navy Nurse, the Philippines, 1942

The Bataan Death March

Okay, you want the story of Bataan?
Well, here's a toilet pit, a narrow slit
of dirt dug by the roadside, and in it
a man so weak he can't climb out again,
he slips back in. And now the Japanese
order you, *Cover up the pit and bury
him there alive.* You just do it, and very
quickly you learn to let emotions freeze
inside your mind. You learn, if you must go,
go in your pants and keep on walking. Stop,
collapse, or step aside and you'll be shot.
You walk all day, pass out at night and do
what you must do. A Filipino man
is giving rice balls to American
prisoners, till an officer cuts off
his head. You walk through beauty, fields and crops
and little huts, through horror, past the corpse
of a raped girl, legs spread, dress pulled up,
a bamboo stake stuck in her privates. No
water for days, no food. They'll make you stand
by a stream side, your thirst a wildfire, and
when one man falls face down to drink, you know
what they will do. Off with his head. That's pure
evil, real evil. But we watched, kept still,
walked when they told us to walk, knowing that
the buzzard squads come up behind to kill
the ones who fall and don't get up. I'm sure
the wild dogs in the area got fat.

American Soldier, Bataan, the Philippines, April, 1942

Rhinestones and Cologne

They got us at Corregidor that June
of '42. Some gave in to the stress,
gave up, blank-faced, but I'd look at the moon,
the same one as at home, and I'd obsess
about such things. Forget the rats, the snake
coiled on my mat, the sores, all that is moot
if with your brain you can eat chocolate cake,
filet miñon, champagne, or kiss a beaut
right on the lips, like Barrymore and Garbo.
I got the guys to join me in a play
in which I played a Chaplin hobo.
It kept us living for another day.
Imagination's a cheap jewel, rhinestone,
but I say if life stinks put on cologne.

American POW, Cabanatuan Prison Camp, the Philippines,
1942-45

Camp Morale

We fed on rumors, even as our bellies
fed on themselves. They gave us hope
when all we saw was dying buddies,
beatings and work, no sign of help.
The ones who gave up, they went limp.
They had no life inside, no fire.
They closed into themselves. The camp
had fences of electric wire
and sometimes you would see these guys
walk up to the fence and grab on.
I don't care what anyone says,
when you decide to die, you're gone,
like this one guy I knew. "To hell
with it, I've had enough," he said,
and rolled away to face the wall.
Five minutes later he was dead.

American POW, Cabanatuan Prison Camp, the Philippines,
1942-45

Beriberi

I guess I was the strongest of all us
at Camp O'Donnell or among the strong
at least, though I fell sick. Before too long
I swelled so big I was like a white walrus,
flopping around. I couldn't really move.
I couldn't even fit onto the bed.
But I was lucky. There were thousands dead
from strange disease, pneumonia above
the rest, or beriberi, what I had.
Your kidneys stop and you can't process fluid.
I was a muffin, was puffed up so bad
my testicles were softballs. I got through it.
I couldn't fit in pants till I got well.
I swelled, and swelled, and swelled. Now that was hell.

American POW, Camp O'Donnell Prison Camp, the Philippines,
1942-45

Survivor

Deep in the ship big shells were piled
like grey, finned tuna fish, and though the fuses
had been removed, they scared me. Like a child
everything scared me then. I have excuses.
To be afraid is eminently sane
when you must charge with just a bayonet
against machine-gun fire, when sudden pain
hits and you fall through dark against a wet
soft thing and feel its flesh reeking and cold
while air-cooled guns were hammering Kan-*kan*!
Kan-*kan*! Kan-*kan*! with bullets big as rolled
hot towels. Can you blame me because I ran
and hid? The brave ones didn't make it home.
They were shot full of holes like honeycombs.

Japanese Soldier, Bataan, the Philippines, 1942

Horse Cock and Cheese

I ate the cheese, I ate horse cock
(that's what we called cold cuts), same chow
as all the men, avoiding talk
of Jesus Christ. It's not like now.
In those days I could not admit
to other folk I was a Jew.
I'd huddle in a trench, sky lit
red with death, by brothers who knew
nothing of me. I'd give my praise
to God. I killed. I tried to earn
another day alive. I slogged through soup.
Was I not good enough to raise
a gun by you? Why not just burn
me up and turn me into soap?

American Marine, Guadalcanal, Solomon Islands, 1942-43

Reversal at the Battle of Midway

The lookout yelled "Hell-divers" and I saw
three black planes plunging towards my head. We shot
a frantic burst from the guns, but it was
too late. Their bombs were off. I knew to toss
my body to the deck and quickly crawl
behind rolled mattresses we used to keep
safe from the shrapnel. Like a dark skylark
diving to snatch a fly, from a high peak
above the cloud-cover, the next plane came
screaming. A flash, strange blast of warm air, then
a startling quiet. We'd been tricked. They'd hid
high up and sent planes skimming low to make
us waste a flight. Then we were in the net,
fueled planes on deck, nothing to do but die.

Japanese Sailor, Aircraft Carrier Akagi, Midway Atoll, 1942

Lou the Card

Here comes Lou, walking briskly down the beach,
exaggerating his salute and grinning
that grin that says he just don't care. A peach
of a guy, Lou. Next thing I know he's spinning
fast all the way around, a yo-yo twirling
on a string. Then he falls down to earth, dead
but looking at me still, bright red unfurling
in a tide pool. He was shot through the head.
He always cracked us up, cracked eggs into
the sergeant's helmet when he napped, would tell
the wildest pornographic jokes. When I
told him first time he caught a bullet, "Lou,
you got a hole in you, sit still!" "Yeah, well,"
he smiled, "you shoulda seen the other guy."

Doctor, U.S. Marine Rangers, Tarawa, 1943

Massacre Bay

People forget about Massacre Bay
on Attu in the Aleutians. The Japs
was dug in there in caves, no way
to clean those rat nests out but flame. Perhaps
we lost some men we didn't need to, cooking
them good with flamethrowers. Smarter to wait
for them to starve. Later on, I was looking
for hand grenades or flags, for stuff to take.
All the dead bodies was froze solid, so
they didn't stink too much. I found a letter
in a Jap soldier's pocket. Translated,
it said, "We're all too sick to eat. There's no
food anyway. Soon they will come. It's better.
I love you. When you read this, I'll be dead."

Navy Crew Chief and Top Turret Gunner, Aleutian Islands,
1943

The Island of Women

Well, here's the thing you gotta know, we was
eighteen years old, just kids; it was a fine
adventure. Bodies didn't bother us.
All you would think about was girls to wine
and dine. Yeah, right! To share C-rations with,
more like. Or share your bed: a Quonset hut
cold as a witch's tit. Still, that's the myth,
the soldier-lover, and I'll tell you what,
the captain pumped us up, "Behind each tree
you'll find a girl." Thing was, there was just grass
and ice on that damn island. Trees, my ass!
By this time in the campaign, all the Japs
was dead or starving in their caves, and we
picked through their frosted corpses, in deep freeze
ourselves, complaining, "Where's the girls?" And Cap?
The captain laughed, "Well, boys, they're with the trees."

Navy Crew Chief and Top Turret Gunner, Aleutian Islands,
1943

The Battle for Saipan

They served us steak for breakfast. Then I saw
against the sky the slender island palms
erupt in the bombardment, ripped apart.
We shimmied down from the ship's deck at dawn,

on long rope ladders into landing craft
that pitched and ran aground on coral reefs.
Machine gun fire and phosphorus shell blasts
hit us wading chest deep to the beach.

The Japs had set up trenches and tank traps.
To get our range they'd placed tall bamboo poles
at intervals. They cut us up. At last
we made a beachhead, ducked into fox holes.

Once inland it was like a firing range,
a butcher shop of torn-up men, the air
alive with cries, the spent shell casings, strange
sugary blood smell, white dust everywhere.

We took that island, but the worst of it
was the civilians, who feared our men like death.
Hundreds of them dove right off the cliffs.
Mothers, weeping, held their kids and leapt.

I was Intelligence, spoke Japanese,
but though I called to them on loudspeaker,
"We won't harm you. Don't jump! Surrender, please!"
they thought it was a trick, embraced the air.

They served us steak for breakfast, some fresh flesh
red on the metal plate. That's what you get
before they send you rushing at your death,
tough steak. I ate it, killed, and lived. And yet,

back home, they took our grocery store and land.
And though I signed up, shipped out, fought like hell,
back home, they put my family into camps
as if we weren't American at all.

Japanese American Soldier, M.I.S., Saipan, Mariana Islands,
1944

The Man I Left Alive

moved in the rocks with inching fingers
among the feathery tall palms
and picked us off. We felt such anger
we wanted to charge in, but "Calm
yourselves," the captain said, "We'll kill
this sniper." Scarecrows made of stuffed
uniforms, rifles for bones, filled
with grass and fronds seemed just enough
like men to make him waste his fire
and show us where to creep. One spurt
right in the gut. I left him there,
curled like a grub, took his gun for
a trophy. No, it wasn't fair.
What is? He'd die. But first he'd hurt.

American G.I., Tinian, Mariana Islands, 1944

Hero

I pumped gas at the Sinclair while the green
dinosaur grinned at me, wiped windshields, spat
and rubbed the squashed bugs off. I was fourteen
and going nowhere, fast. Enough of that!
It was the biggest thing around and I
was sure as hell not going to miss the show.
I lied about my age and got to go.
I never thought that maybe I would die
until I saw the kamikazes dive
straight at our ship. We whacked 'em from the sky
and took some shitty island. It is laugh-
aloud stupid, this hero stuff. Just live!
Leyte, Saipan, who cares? No. I won't cry.
I won't. It was the high point of my life.

U.S. Marine, Leyte, the Philippines, 1944

The Drowned Man

The picket ship went round and round
as in a dance and shells caught dawn
on fire. Flames spilled from the steel rind
like juice from a cracked fruit, then down
she went, bow pointing up to Heaven,
and drowned the flames and men inside.
The submarine offered safe haven,
but I come from the samurai,
and though I was among the five
who were thrown off the deck into
the sea, I didn't want to live
a captive. I'd rather sink through
that ocean's hidden womb and curl
like abalone in those strange
waters, with eyes like clouded pearl,
I had my pride. I would not change.
But they would not leave me to drown
and open water didn't hide
me, so I swam off and went down
with a wood bucket on my head.

Japanese Sailor, South of the Bonin Islands, 1944

Beach Landing, Iwo Jima

They didn't shoot at us. A silent scene
until we clogged the beach, and then—all hell,
potato masher hand grenades, machine
gun fire, artillery. I swear each shell
passed close enough you could reach up and catch
it like a ball. I crawled across black sand,
and used each corpse for cover. Don't attach
yourself, is what I learned. Push it down and
crawl in a hole. Go numb, and you'll survive,
maybe, as I survived. I didn't hate
the man who charged me with his bayonet.
I crouched and shot him dead so I could live.
But the photo in his helmet cut my heart.
A child, smiling at me. And then I wept.

U.S. Marine, Iwo Jima, 1945

Grace under Pressure

When the potato masher hand grenade
flew in the hollow, Mark, the quiet boy,
looked at me with such sorrow. Then he lay
down on the thing. He knew his death would buy
our lives, and so he spent it all, just tossed
his future in the pot like a big spender
in Vegas. Damn him, who can pay that loss
off? I can't. "Neither borrower nor lender"
was what my pop taught me. For what he gave
with rag doll arms spread wide when the bomb blew
him off the earth, I kissed his dirty face,
closed his dead eyes. I knew I had to live
my life a cleaner way, the way he flew
into the sky (before he fell). With grace.

U.S. Marine, Iwo Jima, 1945

The Cave

I was the torch man, and I liked it, strange
as that is to admit. It was the worst
thing in the world. I'd sneak up into range
and throw a flame in, just a burst. A burst
is all it takes. It sucks the oxygen
and then they burn alive or suffocate.
My mouth still tastes that taste, burnt flesh. Back then,
I felt nothing. I did my job. No hate,
no nothing. The men liked me, called me Hot Shot.
But it meant nothing when the Nips would rush
out, clothes on fire and smoking, and we'd shoot
them dead. It meant we lived. Nothing to gush
about. I don't have anything to hide.
Nothing. I shoved it all down deep inside.

U.S. Marine, Iwo Jima, 1945

55

Banzai Charge

The Japanese came at us from the cave,
yelling and waving swords. We mowed them flat
with submachine guns. Well, we only gave
what they were handing out, a good death that
the captain could write home about. This one
kid, though, his face is in my eyes. Today
is nearly sixty years after my gun
was stripped and cleaned and oiled and laid away
and still he's in my eyes, he's in my eyes.
You shoot them any way you have to do.
You couldn't take them prisoner. They'd lie
upon a hand grenade and wait for you,
then it's *ka-blam!* We made sure they were dead,
real dead. We shot survivors in the head.

U.S. Marine, Iwo Jima, 1945

Seeds of Gold

They called me Harvester because each field
of dead Nips gave a crop of souvenirs
for me to gather. Good stuff, if you steeled
yourself to reap it. Still, I cried real tears
when Sergeant Bill took sniper shot right through
the eye. But why should I die, too? I'd fake
an injury, or disappear into
a cave until the fighting stopped, then take
the little metal hammer that I kept
inside my pack and knock the fillings out
of molars and bicuspids. You should see
the bag of teeth I bagged. It wasn't theft.
The dead don't shop. I say, when asked about
my wealth, "I got my start in dentistry."

U.S. Infantryman, Iwo Jima, 1945

The Crew

Mac was a good 'ol boy from Tennessee,
the Sergeant was a South Bronx loan shark,
Slow Jack's a farm boy from New Harmony,
and I was green, still frightened of the dark.
That was our crew. At least, the ones not dead.
Slow Jack kept gold teeth tied up in a sock.
The Sergeant had his legs cut off by Doc
and begged me would I shoot him in the head.
I couldn't do it for him, and his screams
went on all night. Later, I lost this arm.
I still wake up with night sweats and night fears
and see the girl I killed inside my dreams.
Slow Jack is back and working on the farm.
Mac has a necklace made of human ears.

U.S. Marine, Iwo Jima, 1945

War Sickness

I had a deal with Doctor Noburo
that when the fighting got intense he'd say
I had malaria and could not go,
but I was well. The Buddha says the Way
seems wrong to butchers, honor will look stealthy
to thieves, the truth is paradox. Banzai
attacks, bushido, suicide, are healthy
for the brainsick. But I don't want to die
for false beliefs. Of course I know you think
I'm sick with cowardice, that I'm no good.
I say the illness is in you. Why fight,
get shot, get stabbed, get crushed beneath a tank?
I don't believe the Emperor is God.
I don't believe to die in war is right.

Japanese Soldier, Guangxi, China

Yellowbelly

The place I lived then was some trashy shacks
right off the highway. Off the reservation,
they didn't treat us white. I stood attacks
from fists in bars, from Sheriff Jack. Damnation!
You think I cared they called me yellowbelly?
A red-skinned yellowbelly. That's a laugh.
These days I have computers, have a telly
and a flush toilet, a new kind of life.
Back then I had my sense of justice, knew
I wouldn't fight the white man's war. They stuck
me on a train, sent me to jail. Of course
they beat me, thought they'd snap my mind in two,
those gung ho big goon guards, called me "red fuck,"
thought they could break my spirit. Not this horse.

Conscientious Objector, New Mexico

The Death of Private K

The men were thin as bamboo sticks, as light
as infants, faltering on thin bird legs
with deep-set eyes that shone out strangely bright.
But Private K was strong, not one who lags
behind, and though his lower half had turned
dark purple from the gunshot through his thigh,
he kept up for three days, till the wound burned
too much. We left, said we'd return, but I
refused at first to go back and take care
of him. "He'll leak when he is captured," said
the captain. "You must go." I couldn't bear
it, but went, hoping that I'd find him dead.
He wept and smiled at me, "You kept your word!"
Then I wept, too. And killed him with my sword.

Japanese Soldier, Luzon, the Philippines, 1945

The Burma Road

We called that road Corpse Way for all the men
dead by its side. We struggled on that road,
all young men in our twenties but all bowed
like stooped old men. I saw a Buddha then.
No, it was a soldier deep in thought
while the men scrapped for rice. He watched this show
then pulled the rifle trigger with one toe
and blew his head apart. Two soldiers fought
to get his boots, since ours were rotted out.
I saw two lovers then. No, it was just
two men embracing there by the roadside.
One pulled the pin; they blew. I saw this route
was death, the road of nausea, path of rust,
and walked on it: the way of suicide.

Staff Sergeant, Japanese Engineering Regiment, Burma, 1945

The Cannibals

We all suspicioned something from the way
the air smelt in the cave. I see again
that sight, stuck in my eyes. No way to say
it but they ate their own. Well, you can train
a man to kill straight as an avenue,
to follow rules, but stomach must be filled.
If you don't eat then death will sure eat you.
I guess that's how they conscienced it. I killed,
but never took no pleasure in it. Cry
much as you want, you're stuck in this damn place
and it'll make you do things, by and by.
You'll fry a cat in coconut, you'll face
what you can do and say that you don't care,
but smell it in your mind, burnt flesh, burnt hair.

U.S. Infantryman, New Guinea, 1942-1944

White Pig, Dark Pig

I didn't rape the women, didn't lust
for their dark flesh, not like you think. I dreamed
of food, not sex. A man does what he must
to live. I ate dark breasts and brains. It seemed
normal, almost. I met some soldiers near
the camp. They carried a cooked human arm
from a white pig (that is, a prisoner
from the West). They were lucky, with a farm
of endless white pigs to roast up. But we
had to track down the dark ones hiding, and
we starved. At last we drew lots, and the one
who lost we'd eat. The loser tried to flee.
He'd been my friend. I shot him with my gun,
then wept. I got his leg and his left hand.

Japanese Soldier, New Guinea, 1942-1944

Strange Vigil on the Field One Night

He fell into my hole, stone dead and shot
right through the eye. I had to look. That hole.
I can't stop seeing it. We both turned cold,
lying all night in the foxhole. I fought
to stay awake because the Japs would steal
in under cover of the dark and knife
you in your sleep. His good eye, open, life-
like, gazed up at the billion stars. To peel
my lids apart each time they closed, oh man,
was murder. At dawn, before I climbed out free
from that damp hole I folded him up well
in his wool blanket, tucked it carefully
over his head, under his feet, and then
in that rude grave I left him where he fell.

U.S. Marine, Okinawa, 1945

The Dead

Yeah, it's the stink, the stink of death,
that is the worst smell you can smell.
The dead were there, with blood and earth
on them, along the road for miles,
laid out. They sent me for a wrench
and so I hoofed it between those
dead on the way out. But that stench.
Can't get it out your clothes.
To keep from passing death a man
will walk out of his way about
halfway from here to Rocky Gap.
I walked around, that's what I mean
to say. I walked a long ways out
of the straight way when I came back.

American Soldier, Okinawa, 1945

Mass Suicide, Okinawa

They said Americans were demons,
rapists and cannibals who'd slice
off lips and leave a red hole screaming,
chop fingers, noses, ears, and sluice
the blood into a metal cup
to drink. They said mass suicide
was preferable to giving up,
and so the women neatly tied
their hair, the men looked round for blades,
sharp scythes and knives, and stuck
their necks and wrists to free the blood.
I battered mother with a stick
till she stopped moving, then was sick.
The bodies all were gathered in
one meadow, field mice in a sack,
my sister strangled with a string,
brother with skull cracked by a stone,
the village, dead. I rolled around,
out of my head. What had we done?
I left that place and went to ground,
starving, ghost-hunted, living in caves.
I can't believe what I believed.
The streams were colored red for days.
I drank from those death streams, and lived.

Village Boy, Okinawa, 1945

White Fear

They thought they were the big white men, could take
the Japs like shooting monkeys in the zoo.
Those tiny men were not quite men, would break
like yellow eggs. Uh-huh. They feared us, too.
The white men wouldn't let us near their whores.
But I kept flirting. I was a young blade.
They made black soldiers into stevedores
and cooks and servants since they were afraid
of giving guns to men they wouldn't let
piss next to them, or sit next to their wives.
To keep the women off us young black males
they said we howled at night. Said we had tails!
I cooked their food. And I kept flirting. Bet
on it. You think I'd stop? Not on their lives.

African-American U.S. Marine Corps Messman, Okinawa,
1945

The Doll

Let me hold the doll my daughter
used to sleep with in my lap, and let
the glass of life be shattered.
I will eat bean curd and rice
and carry charms and flakes
of dried bonito with me in the cockpit
and fly into the dome of heaven.
Let the clouds part like hair and let
the sky open to me, and then
the way a cherry blossom releases
from its branch let me release
from life and fall into their ship
beautifully, let the fire open
like a flower, let steam and smoke
bloom, and let me do my duty
for today, which is to die.

Kamikaze Pilot, Okinawa, 1945

The Ball Turret Gunner

Inside this ball of magic glass
they put a tiny man, with guns,
a sphere of battered plexiglass
where I am naked to the sun.
It's like a toy world, miniature,
except with death—a sweet white flock
of lamblike clouds where colors tear
the blue with tracer fire, black flak.
A pilot close enough to knife
me with his gaze dives like a seal
and I'm the shark. My two guns speak,
then stutter, and he keeps his life.
In the blue dome, time congeals.
He swims off slowly, bleeding smoke.

American Gunner, B-17 Flying Fortress

The Underwater Ship

When the torpedo hit it was the fist
of God. It chopped the bow right off, but we
were under way, scooping in water, twist-
ing screws still turning, till the open sea
opened up its mouth and sucked us down.
No time to radio an SOS,
no time for anything but jump, or drown.
After two days we were in such distress,
such thirst, some sailors let their heads dip forward,
and drowned. And other men began to mass
hallucinate, "The ship's still here, oh Lord!
It's here below the waves. Come get a glass
of milk, get some tomato juice, for love
of God!" then slipped out of their vests, and dove.

Crewman, U.S.S. Indianapolis, 1945

The Shape of Fear

That's when the sharks showed up. Oh, God! I called,
"What's that?" I'd felt one brush against my shins.
My heart was like to bust. And then, appalled,
I saw them moving there, a flash of dorsal fins,
a swirl of white disturbance in the waves.
You know how fishing bobbers jerk when fish
strike them? Men died that way. That's all I'll say.
I swear by dusk each little splash and swish
became a thrashing, gnashing shark inside
my mind. Yet in that mental night I dreamed
somehow. I slept, slipping into the wide
cosmos of exhaustion. Till someone screamed.
And then I floated helpless in that dark,
imagining the sharks, the goddamn sharks.

Crewman, U.S.S. Indianapolis, 1945

THE BOMB

Holocausts of Water and Fire

You can't say I liked killing kids.
I told myself: treat beasts as beasts.
It's most regrettable but true.
Think of Pearl Harbor and their murder
of prisoners. The A-bomb spoke
a language they would understand,
I reasoned. But I fear machines
have outpaced morals; when this race
is done there'll be no reasons left.
We're termites in the planet's crust.
We bore too deeply in the earth
to find its secrets and there'll be
a reckoning before we're done.

The Hebrew visionaries said
the world would die in holocausts
of water and of fire, first rains,
and Noah and his fabled Ark,
and then the world would die in flames
and spin through space inert and dark.
The fire holocaust has come.
We made a bomb more terrible
than any bomb in history.
It was the worst thing ever made.
Monstrous. But it could be of use.

Harry Truman, Washington, D.C., 1945

Gunner's Perspective

I only saw Japan in miniature as
I shot at zeros from the bomber's balls
(our name for the machine gun turrets
under the plane). I wished we'd killed them all.
We tried. First high explosive bombs to smash
their homes to kindling, then, so they'd combust,
oil sticks and fire bombs. A bed of ash.
That's all was left of Tokyo. Like a beast,
a savage, I was happy as the tiny
city caught flame. And I escaped my fate,
secretly glad each time a buddy's shiny
plane fell. I'll go soon–cancer–years too late.
Soon I'll be among the honored dead,
each one of whom thought, *No, take him instead.*

Ball Turret Gunner, B-29 Bomber, Tokyo, 1945

Fireflies over Tokyo

We heard the sirens screech and then the sky
turned bleeding, awful, red. Some kind of bomb
shattered the houses, then like fireflies
the spinning oil sticks dropped. It was napalm.
We fled as flames splashed out from windows, ran
from flames that ate the oxygen, ran through
the streets as fire stuck to our clothes. A man
fell underfoot, was trampled. No one knew
where we should run among the roasted dead.
Some people jumped in the Sumida River,
and though we saw them cook alive like herrings,
"How beautiful," my mother said, as silver
needles unstitched the sky, with liquid red
reflections streaming underneath their wings.

Housewife, Tokyo, 1945

The Trinity Test

We all came out to Trinity
(the name was Oppenheimer's bright
idea—for some fellow's poem,
Batter my heart, three-person'd God,
that one) and right by base camp we
lay in the dirt, ten miles from ground
zero, and watched the shot through dark
glass like they use in welders' helmets.

I couldn't look at first but felt
heat on my temple. When I turned
at last, through the dark welding glass
I saw ballooning up a flaming
planet that glowed inside dull red
and folded in upon itself
like bread dough in a mixing bowl.
The earth held it by a dark stem.

Somebody said, "My God!" and we
all felt relief. We cheered and went
about and shook each other's hands.
And then the ground shock hit us hard,
and the sound echoing back and
forth from the hills for a long time.
A hush. Someone said, "Well, it worked."
And then we talked of other things.

Scientist, Trinity Test, White Sands, New Mexico, 1945

The Day of Days

I bet you think you know about the test
out in the desert, how we didn't know
whether our boy would fizzle or would blow,
bet you were shocked by people charred like toast.
But here's what you don't know about the Bomb:
we thought it might ignite the atmosphere,
set off a chain reaction and go on
to burn all life from earth. That was our fear.
There was a chance it might combust creation
from here right to the throne of God. It might.
Or else it might not work. Of course the nation
needed the Bomb, but we knew that that day
might turn all nations into dust and light.
We knew. And yet we did it anyway.

Scientist, Trinity Test, White Sands, New Mexico, 1945

The Pilot's Tale

In the plane's glass nose the whole sky
lit up the beautifulest blue
you ever seen, bright blue, but I
did not react when the bomb blew.
Not right away. Then I turned round
and saw the cloud of boiling dust
bubbling upwards from the ground
where I guess Hiroshima must
have been, and felt the silver fillings
electrify my teeth. They sent
the chills all through me, boots to hair.
We wiped 'em out. And as for killing
the ones they say were innocent—
that's their tough luck for being there.

Pilot, Enola Gay, Hiroshima, 1945

The Bombardier's Tale

I called out "Bomb away," but didn't know
what kind of bomb it was we dropped that day.
A minute later the shock wave rocked the plane
and then Paul banked us so that we could see
the ground like boiling tar, a mass of rubble
that flowed in all directions outwards to
the docks and mountains. I'm awful sorry
lots of people died, but it was war.
I don't feel guilty. Through nine miles of sky
no one could tell a soldier from a child.

Bombardier, Enola Gay, Hiroshima, 1945

Morning in Hiroshima

A morning beautiful and sweet,
and clad in undershirt and drawers
I watched my garden through the doors,
the shifting, sunlit, shimmering leaves.
Then the stone lamp lit up white like
a bright magnesium flare. I plucked
a large glass shard out of my neck
and looked at it. I called my wife
as the house sagged and began falling,
everything tumbling to the floor.
I ran out through the house next door,
tripped on something and fell sprawling.
My foot had caught on a man's head.
"Excuse me, please! Excuse me, please!"
I cried to him hysterically.
There was no answer. He was dead,
his body crushed beneath a large
red gate. I ran through the street bare.
Where were my shirt and underwear?
Our city was on fire, and our
neighbors walked around like ghosts,
their arms held straight out from their bodies.
Then suddenly I saw their bodies
had been charred black, that they were hold-
ing their arms out to stop the sting
of friction. Now a flaming man
ran by. I couldn't understand
what thing had happened, what strange thing.

Doctor, Hiroshima, 1945

Roast Fish and Sweet Yams

The bright light stuck into my eyes
like twenty dozen pins. Back then
I was four, but today I'm ten.
We ran into the street, and I
could see my dad was roasted like
a fish above his waist. Some friend
put oil on him. I thanked him in
my heart. My mom got sick and died.

Back home, everything was broken
but we lived there. At two A.M.
one night my grandmother awoke
when dad called out for some sweet yams.
"Very well," she said, and put them on.
"It's done," she said. He didn't move.
I touched him to see what was wrong.
His skin felt cold. And then I knew.

Boy, Hiroshima, 1945

White Bones

Mother was burned into white bones
while praying at our Buddhist altar.
I can't recall her face, but some
days at the painted wooden post
that marks her grave I pray to mother.
The post is silent and I go
home, leaving her some pretty flowers.
I was just five. I don't remember.

Girl, Hiroshima, 1945

Chopsticks

I had my chopsticks to my mouth
when the big bang and the sharp flash
hit us. Things fell inside the house.
My dad had glass stuck in his back.
We ran outside through flames and dust.
My grandma ran into a post and died.
I think my father must have touched
some poison thing. Later, he died.
I tried to cross the railroad track
but it burned me, so I jumped back.
At the river people were burned black
and crying, "Water!" But those who drank
the water died. Later, my sister's
left thumb was ready to drop off,
and then a boil was on my brother's
head and if you pressed it slightly, pus
oozed out. My mom could only lie
in bed. I felt so sad. My mom,
she had a baby boy and died
with him. Only his head was born.

Girl, Hiroshima, 1945

Snapshot

It was as if someone had shot a flash
off inches from my eyes. It was white, white,
and stung my cheeks as if I had been slapped
hard in the face. I must have lost some time,
because I woke up in a shattered house.
Then stumbling down the street, I heard the people
crying "Help," but I could not help, and now
I passed by a stalled streetcar of dead people
and touched the yellow burns across my face
and body. Odd. The flesh was hanging free.
I tried to pat my skin back into place.
Some people were so charred I could not see
if they were lying face down or on their backs.
They didn't look like human beings. But they
were still alive. I thought, who could do that?
And then my heart filled up with bitter hate.
People lay along the rivers screaming.
The sky was red. Hiroshima was burning.

Girl, Hiroshima, 1945

The Schoolgirl's Tale

My friend's red mouth was open wide
in fright. She couldn't speak a word,
her teeth knocked out. I saw the blood
splashed on my breast. It wasn't mine.
Another friend was crushed and cough-
ing blood. I tried but couldn't help her.
And then I saw three naked soldiers,
their skin seared black and hanging off.
About this time my girlfriend died.
I saw the freight trains full of coal
ignite and blaze up high and boil
with fire. They lit the hill all night,
and when at last the red sun dawned
on the dead city, the black smoke
still steamed out from the bodies broken
on the sidewalks I walked. I saw
a child cry out and shake its mother's
dead arm. I saw a black thing then
which anyone would think was dead.
I heard it whisper "Water, water."

Schoolgirl, Hiroshima, 1945

A Black Rain Fell

First came the flare. Then, it was strange,
I saw blue morning-glories bloom
across the sky. Blue clouds. Next came
the heat wave, so hot the room
was like a fever. Something snapped,
I don't know what; maybe the air
expanding cracked the walls. The path
outside was filled with people, bare
and silent, running from the flames.
The city was half dark with smoke
and half was clear and light. Black rain
was falling. Like wet tar it stuck
to everything, to leaves and trees,
and couldn't be washed off. It stuck
to skin and clothes and hands and feet.
It stuck, and everything turned black.

Weather Man, Hiroshima, 1945

The Blue Flash

Just like a train sparking the rails
the blue flash hit, and then a gale
blew me into the next room.
Strange black, deep black. Then I came to
beneath roof tiles and red soil,
stood up and looked at all the homes
collapsed as far as I could see.
Someone shouted "Help!" below my feet.
Next door I saw my neighbor's dad
standing dazed and almost nude.
His skin was peeling off in strips
and hanging from his fingertips.
Fire swept us toward the river.
You couldn't see the water
for all the bodies floating dead.
A strange rain fell in fat black drops.
There was a woman who we tried
to help, trapped beneath a beam, alive.
But the fire came, and then, hands clasped,
we deeply bowed to her and left.
We had no choice. Despite the years
I still sit back-to-wall in fear,
glass windows fill me with fright,
and I can't stand sparks or lightning.

Teenage Boy, Hiroshima, 1945

Rosie the Riveter

I do recall the atom bomb,
and I recall how glad we were
that day. Because the men were gone
to war, me and the gals repaired
planes at the base. Some days we'd rivet,
or else we'd clean the glass and blood
from out the cockpits, knowing that
it could be from a friend or loved
one, that was hard, and then we sent
them out again. How did I feel
about the Japs? Well, by the end
of that big war I could've kneeled
them in a row and shot them all
myself. That's why we all were dancing
when the bomb dropped. That's why we all
threw parties. Everyone was dancing.

Riveter, American Airbase, El Segundo, California, 1945

Not Enough

Just don't give me that peacenik crap.
Enough good men are dead and gone.
My George here would have died, for one,
and one dead Jap is one good Jap.
So I thank God and Truman for
the Bomb. So far as I'm concerned,
they got exactly what they earned.
We should've dropped a couple more.

American Nurse, Corpus Christi, Texas, 1945

The Pit

The men who volunteered to cut off heads
were shocked by Hiroshima, and by the burned
cities. I helped because my wife was dead.
She burned alive. The captured pilots earned
this death. In a blank field, stripped to their shorts.
they watched us, blear-eyed. I think they knew it
before they saw the hole to hold their corpses.
We put on blindfolds, kneeled them by the pit.
I killed four, with a borrowed sword. To strike
just right is difficult. The neckbone stops
the blade. But Satano in one fast stroke
cut his off clean. We tried Karate chops
on them for practice, buried head and trunk
below the shallow dirt. Then we got drunk.

Japanese Officer, Western Army Headquarters, Fukuoka,
Japan, 1945

Wartime Medicine

We hated them and thought them less than human,
but they were useful while they were not dead.
We wanted to find out just what would happen
when we dissected them alive. Truman
had firebombed the city and we fled
and hated pilots. They were less than human.
We wouldn't amputate the limbs of true men,
take out their livers, measure how they bled.
We wanted justice, and to find what happens
when you bisect the living lungs. We knew when
they watched us paralyzed with drugs and dread
they hated us. Thoughtless, they ceased to be men
as their blood drained out, and their skin turned blue, and
the tin table filled up with parts turned red.
We wanted to find justice and what happens
when you cut circles in the skull, unscrew them,
then poke a knife into the opened head.
We hated them. We thought them less than human.
So we found out exactly what would happen.

Doctor, Anatomy Department, Kyushu University, 1945

Milk Run

We thought the raid was just a milk run,
but we hit black flak once we shed
our load and watched it drop like rain,
and I saw Al's red chest and dead
white eyes and jumped as the plane spun
off. I was the youngest one, a babe
in arms. That's why I tried to run.
But that was all a hopeless stab
in the dark. See, where could I run
that wouldn't be Japan? They caught
me in some kind of old-style ruin
and I gave up. Should I have fought
them all? Come on. Then later, in
the camp they put me in a cell
right next to Cap, God bless him,
and we whispered all night to tell
what news we knew through the bars. "Hey,
where's Tom? Where's so and so?" I asked.
It kills me what he had to say:
no one but me got out the back
of that damn plane. We lived with lice
and open sores that wouldn't heal
and only little bites of rice
to eat, with giant rats, and holes
that let in light and rain. They made
us piss and crap in a wood pot.
They beat us every day. We faced
our deaths because we wouldn't talk.
The officers would threaten to
slice off our heads with samurai

swords. I don't blame them, much. To do
what the Japs did–it was the times.
But gee whiz, when the A-bomb set
us free, it was "Hip, hip, hooray!"
hats in the air and no regrets.
Yessiree, that was one grand day.

American Prisoner of War, Aomori Prison Camp, Japan, 1945

Nagasaki Drop

We tried to fry the Japanese alive
in Tokyo, fireblasted every city,
almost, but left some virgin. They were pretty
lucky, they thought. Then we nuked them. We give
excuses but the truth is we was just
young bucks. The army told us what to think
and do, then we did it. I'm one to thank
for Nagasaki, though it was a bust
at first 'cause of cloud cover. Nagasaki
was our third choice, and it was luck decided
where that great jellyfish of light would swell
into the sky. Luck, or weather, divided
the clouds and showed the city. And then hell
on earth ended the war. Now that was lucky.

Crewman, Bock's Car, Nagasaki, 1945

Children

You look at me and see a strange bald man
talking to children in the garden. Well,
adults can learn something from children, can
understand hate and pettiness, the hell
we've made of earth. Their nature is not good.
They squabble over candy, toys and caste.
I've heard it said, "Be like a child." Why should
I play while the world waits for the bomb blast?
I've heard, "The atom bomb will bring us peace.
Ash children, firestorms, the poison breeze,
will nauseate us like a greasy feast
so that we'll learn to turn away and fast."
A child who eats until he's going to burst,
will stop—but only while his stomach hurts.

Mahatma Gandhi, 1945

Krishna's Chariot

I woke one August day and read
in big, black headlines of the death
of a great city. In one breath
I felt elation and then dread.
We live at the edge of mystery,
surrounded by it. The great flash
has led us to a mountain pass.
Beyond there is a different country.
Though Truman says the Bomb brought peace
the scientists I know are frightened,
frightened for their lives, and frightened
for yours. I was there at its release
and when I saw the toadstool whirl
up into heaven, I thought of Krishna's
battlefield words in Bhagavad-Gita:
"Now I am death, destroyer of worlds."

J. Robert Oppenheimer, 1945

ENDINGS

On the Day Japan Surrenders

We hold a swim meet in the pond and walk
there naked, some of us with homemade poles
we'll use as swords if the shy pond fish balk
at the sharp hook. We are just boys. The roles
we are to carry, warrior, defender
of the home islands, husband, worker, father,
we shed as easily as clothes. Like tender
fish-meat field-roasted on the spits we gather
from bamboo stands, we are white meat well-browned
by summer sun and hardly care a bit
about the whale-like gun-gray battleship
passing offshore, winged shadows on the ground
from pretty silver bombers, cities lit
by napalm. I shout out, "Time for a dip!"

Boy, Meijima, 1945

The Thin Man

I ripped my ration card and screamed,
then kissed the thin man standing next
to me. He leapt away. It seemed
everyone was jumpy—effects
of wartime—and he hadn't heard
the news. The war was over! When
I told him, first he looked real hard
to see if I was joking, then
grabbed me and kissed me back. We were
married for forty years. A whole
lifetime. He was such a slim wire
back then. He climbed up a phone pole
shouting, "We've won the war!" The street
erupted. I loved his fat grin,
so I shucked shoes and with bare feet
shimmied up the pole next to him.

Army Nurse, West Virginia, 1945

Nonconformist

People round here went nuts. The tire drives,
victory gardens, sugar scarce as gold,
it was the biggest thing in their small lives.
The boys were off at war, so just the old,
the gossips, busybodies, stayed in town,
and they kept busy sticking noses in
my business. Mrs. Johnston would knock down
my door almost to get me to give in
and give away my pots and pans. They'd sit
in the clock tower watching through the nights
for Jap planes over Kansas. I drew flak
for keeping lights on during blackouts. Pack
mentality. I didn't care a bit.
On V-J Day I shut my door and lights.

World War I Vet, Kansas, 1945

The Power of a God

The day we turned about and changed our course
and sailed for home, the biggest goddamn storm
you ever saw rolled in, and like a worm
I looked up at the chariot and horse
of some Greek god with lightning in his hair
who thundered and tossed spears of light at us.
Well, that's my fantasy. It was a fuss
made up of cold and hot layers of air,
precipitation, electricity.
And though the sky turned black and though the sea
tossed us like salad till men cried in wonder
and though I like the notion of gods, too,
we don't need gods to make the heavens thunder.
On earth with men a howitzer will do.

U.S. Marine, 3rd Marine Division, Iwo Jima

Farewell to Arms

"The world breaks every one and afterward
many are stronger at the broken places."
I read that in a book. What each man faces
in war is that we're animals with words
to comfort us, like "glory, courage, hallow,"
and the best cuss words almost as obscene,
though "fuck" at least is somewhat comforting
when all those other words seem fucking hollow.
On ship, I read a lot of Hemingway,
a curled up bookworm on my narrow bunk.
And I agree with what he had to say,
that prayer, honor, all that's so much bunk,
no fate to blame or fight with just your fists.
No God. All thinking men are atheists.

Sonarman, 1st Class, Retired, Fresno, California

The Perfect Life

I had the perfect life—big house
and gardens, servants who would cook
and wash and do for me, a horse
to ride, a loving family. They took
my life from me, took me to prison
camp and then later to the brothel.
They laughed at us with such derision
when we protested. It was awful,
what they did, thirty men a night,
month after month. They took my name,
called me White Lily. We deserved
apologies, got none. My fight?
To make them own up to their shame,
and what they did, and how we served.

Sex Slave for the Japanese Army, Indonesia

The Factory

I was thirteen when soldiers kidnapped me.
I crouched down in the truck, silent and trembly.
One man said, "You're off to a factory,"
then laughed. I thought I'd work on an assembly
line, and made peace with it. What a cruel trick.
It was a factory where women made
sex with their bodies. They'd line up to stick
me like they'd stick a bayonet's steel blade
into a prisoner, while men banged at
the door, too frantic to wait turns. And that
is why I swelled like a balloon with pus
and bled so much I lost my uterus.
Look at me. Old, still sick. I have no one.
I live alone and I will die alone.

Sex Slave for the Japanese Army, Korea

War Games

That's when I knew I wouldn't date Spence, when
he told me he was proud of breaking men,
like this old soldier who was a bit weird.
Spence bragged how even though his buddy feared
the guy for what he'd done in war, this vet
who lived alone, they cracked him. While his frat
bro drove the pickup, Spence leaned out to get
the guy's mailbox. He smashed it with a bat.
The crash blew the vet back in time, the wound
inside his mind torn open, and he sat
shaking beneath the desk. That's where they found
him three days later, hunched in his own shit,
in his own urine. He was put away.
Spence laughed, "The man was fucked up anyway."

Young Woman, Yacolt, Washington

The Man Who Won the War

Grandfather never spoke about the war
but people say he won it, worked for Boeing
inventing ways to speed production for
the flying fortresses. The young men going
to die in planes could be replaced, but not
the planes, not fast enough. He didn't choose
to be the man who won the war. He taught,
"Believe in Jesus, just in case." He used
to quiz us, "Why did Xerxes cry?" We said,
"He was the greatest king alive, but knew
within a century he would be dead
and every living person would be too."
Like the young men who went to die in planes.
Like grandfather. He gardened in the rain

in his great backyard jungle, grew tomatoes
as large as bombs. I always wondered what
he put in them, this millionaire with clothes
he bought at Goodwill, this Harvard man cut
from Southern, racist cloth, who yet refused
to give them one red cent because no Jew
could get in there. Almost blind, he used
a magnifying glass to peer into
our faces, asking with his awful breath,
"Which one are you?" And yet he still would drive
with all the kids and swerve around our death
while we yelled, "Hit the brakes!" "Watch out!" We lived.
He never flew in planes. Not out of guilt.
It was because he knew how they were built.

Young Woman, Yacolt, Washington

Hindsight

If you ask me, it wasn't worth it, no,
to go and jump from landing craft and rush
that beach and jungle while the mortars blow
about with bullets buzzing but you push
right on, though you can't see who has you in
their sights. No, wasn't worth it, not to me.
The war was nowheres justified. It's a sin
to chop off heads, to gas those Jews, but we
weren't saints. Seems everyone has points of view
but no one has perspective. What it seems
to me ain't nothing like it seems to you,
and what it means is foggy, like in dreams.
The one thing the war taught me was to think
about that bomb. We're always on the brink.

U.S. Marine, Retired, Pensacola, Florida

Home Brew

He never drank a lick before the war
but he came back a fall-down drunk. He said
they'd cook up home brew from potatoes or
from fruit and then get bombed among the dead.
He started slapping me around, and changed
to someone moaning to himself at night,
oh God, oh Mom, a silent man, deranged
inside, his spirit bottled up. One night
last year I woke up with his hands around
my throat. His mouth was moving. He was dreaming.
I thumbed him in the eyes till he came round
and when he understood he broke down weeping.
He put his medals in a box. It's done,
he said, and got a drink. It wasn't done.

Woman, Evansville, Indiana

At the Retirement Home

I've had both knees replaced. I've got a steel
pin in my hip. I don't hear you so good,
but I'm not stupid, son. How would you feel,
surviving the Bataan Death March, no food
for days, no water, and the ones who fell
behind were bayoneted where they lay,
and now you're marching off to death? Real hell
is not old age, though. No, taking away
the rights we died for, saying torture's right,
that's hell. Hand me the iron and those shirts,
would you? Thanks, son. As long as I have fight
in me I'll love this country till it hurts.
And it does. This is worse than what I saw
overseas. Torture. In America.

U.S. Soldier, 194th Armored Regiment, Retired,
Brainerd, Minnesota

Notes on the Poems

These poems were created over a period of fifteen years, based upon myriad sources. Most poems are based upon the author's imagination working upon multiple interviews, letters, and other historical documents, and most of the characters are composite characters, meant to represent a more widely held position, a socio-economic class, a wartime experience or point of view. Thus, the sources listed below are not meant to give an exhaustive set of inspirations for the poems, just a representative set of such sources, so that the reader can get a sense of how the poems originated. Many thanks go to those who helped me with this research, Dr. Caroline Heldman, Joe Siren, the African American Cultural Center of Allendale, SC, and others.

Some of the major online resources I consulted in researching these poems are: The University of Akron History Department Japan Page website: http://www3.uakron.edu/worldciv/japan.htm; What Did You Do in the War, Grandma? An Oral History of Rhode Island Women during World War II Written by students in the Honors English Program at South Kingstown High School http://www.stg.brown.edu/projects/WWII_Women/tocCS.html; The Rutgers Oral History Archives: http://fas-history.rutgers.edu/oralhistory/home.html; Eyewitness to History.com: http://www.eyewitnesstohistory.com/w2frm.htm; "Prisoner of War Camp #1, Fukuoka, Japan, An Insight into Life and Death at a POW Camp in War-time Japan" by Wes Injerd: http://home.comcast.net/~winjerd/POWCamp1.htm; Prisoner of War Oral History Project: Minnesota POWs of the Japanese, World War Two:http://people.csp.edu/saylor/POWproject/POWinterviews Japanese.htm; War in the Pacific National Historical Park, in Guam, with an excellent website at: http://www.nps.gov/wapa/index.htm.

Among the books I consulted are: Bill Adler with Tracy Quinn McLennan, *World War II Letters: A Glimpse into the Heart of the Second World War through the Words of Those Who Were Fighting It*; Thomas B. Allen, *Remember Pearl Harbor: American and Japanese Survivors Tell Their Stories*; Gerald Astor, *Crisis in the Pacific: The Battles for the Philippine Islands by the Men Who Fought Them*; Paul Boyer, *By the Bomb's Early Light: American Thought and Culture at the Dawn of the Atomic Age*; Tom Brokaw, *The Greatest Generation* and *The Greatest Generation Speaks: Letters and Reflections*; Iris Chang, *The Rape of Nanjing: The Forgotten Holocaust of World War II*; City of Nagasaki, *Testimonies of the Atomic Bomb Survivors: A Record of the Devastation of Nagasaki*; Haruko Taya Cook and Theodore F. Cook, *Japan at War: An Oral History*; John W. Dower, *War Without Mercy: Race and Power in the Pacific War*; Yoichi Fukushima, *Children of Hiroshima*; Frank Gibney, ed., and Beth Cary, trans., *Senso: The Japanese Remember the Pacific War*; Michihiko Hachiya, *Hiroshima Diary*; Jintaro Ishida, *The Remains of War: Apology and Forgiveness, Testimonies of the Japanese Imperial Army and Its Filipino Victims*; Lawson Fusao Inada, ed., *Only What We Carry: The Japanese American Internment Experience*; Dai Sil Kim-Gibson, *Silence Broken: Korean Comfort Women*; Robert S. La Forte, Ronald E. Marcello, and Richard L. Himmel, *With Only the Will to Live: Accounts of Americans in Japanese Prison Camps, 1941-1945*; Yvonne Latty, *We Were There: Voices of African American Veterans from World War II to the War in Iraq*; Jon E. Lewis, *The Mammoth Book of Eyewitness World War II: Over 200 First-Hand Accounts from the Six Years that Tore the World Apart*; Rachel Linner, *City of Silence: Listening to Hiroshima*; John T. Mason, Jr., *The Pacific War Remembered: An Oral History Collection*; Richard H. Minear, *Hiroshima: Three Witnesses;* Christopher Paul Moore, *Fighting for America: Black Soldiers—The Unsung Heroes of World War II*; Hiroko Nakamoto, *My Japan: 1930-1951*; Oliver North with Joe Musser, *War Stories II: Heroism in the Pa-*

cific; Patrick K. O'Donnell, *Into the Rising Sun: In Their Own Words, World War II's Pacific Veterans Reveal the Heart of Combat*; Toyofumi Ogura, *Letters from the End of the World: A Firsthand Account of the Bombing of Hiroshima*; Hiroo Onada, *No Surrender: My Thirty-Year War*; Bruce M. Petty, *Voices from the Pacific War: Bluejackets Remember*; The Library of America, *Reporting World War II: Part One, American Journalism 1938-1944*; S.L. Sanger, *Working on the Bomb: An Oral History of WWII Hanford*; Sangmie Choi Schellstede, *Comfort Women Speak: Testimony by Sex Slaves of the Japanese Military*; Gaynor Sekimori, trans., *Hibakusha: Survivors of Hiroshima and Nagasaki*; Mark Selden and Kyoko Selden, *The Atomic Bomb: Voices from Hiroshima and Nagasaki*; Thomas E. Simmons, *Forgotten Heroes of World War II: Personal Accounts of Ordinary Soldiers*; Rex Alan Smith and Gerald A. Meehl, *Pacific War Stories in the Words of Those Who Survived*; Hiroshima Jogakuin High School English Department, *Summer Cloud: A-bomb Experience of a Girls' School in Hiroshima*; Kazuo Tamayana and John Nunneley, *Tales by Japanese Soldiers*; Yuki Tanaka, *Hidden Horrors: Japanese War Crimes in World War II*; John Tateshi, *And Justice for All: An Oral History of the Japanese American Detention Camps*; Lester I. Tenney, *My Hitch in Hell: The Bataan Death March*; Studs Terkel, *"The Good War": An Oral History of World War Two*; E.T. Wooldridge, *Carrier Warfare in the Pacific: An Oral History Collection*; Samuel Hideo Yamashita, *Leaves from an Autumn of Emergencies: Selections from the Wartime Diaries of Ordinary Japanese*.

A note on dating and the order of the poems: because most of the poems in *Tongue of War* are retrospective poems in which the speakers reflect upon particular events in the War in the Pacific, assigning dates to the poems is complicated. Should one date the poem from the approximate time in which the character might have participated in an oral history, or should one date the poem based upon the approximate date of the events being narrated? I have opted for the latter, because it seems more useful to readers to step them through history in roughly chronological fashion. Occasionally, I have left a poem undated or taken a poem out of chronological sequence for the sake of the thematic development of the book.

"ANGEL OF DEATH" and "JACOB'S LADDER" draw from a number of oral histories by American soldiers and sailors stationed at Pearl Harbor, such as "Attack at Pearl Harbor, 1941," Eyewitness to History, www.eyewitnesstohistory.com (1997) and the set of survivors' tales online at "Pearl Harbor Remembered" (http://my.execpc.com/~dschaaf/personal.htms. These two poems, along with "THE BIRDS OF PEARL HARBOR" are set on the battleship Arizona, which was sunk at Pearl Harbor, with a loss of 1,177 men, after a Japanese bomb penetrated and set off the ammunition magazine, causing a disastrous explosion. In "Angel of Death," "Meatballs" is a slang term that American troops used to refer to the sun insignia on the wings of Japanese planes.

"THE FORGE" is a bouts-rimés poem; that is, it uses the same rhyme-words in the same order as another poem (in this case, Seamus Heaney's sonnet "The Forge").

"THEY COULD HAVE GIVEN IT TO US" is roughly based upon an oral history with Itabashi Koshu, "My Blood Boiled at the News," in *Japan at War: An Oral History*, by Haruko Taya Cook and Theodore F. Cook. I was interested in his description of the Japanese point of view at the time. Though he eventually became a Buddhist priest, at the news of Pearl Harbor he and others were filled with patriotic lust for war, and a sense of a wrong being avenged.

"DISAPPEARING ACT" was inspired by an oral history with Ron Veenker, who was raised in a Frisian community in South Dakota, though some elements of the poem come from other oral histories. The interview appears in Studs Terkel's *The*

Good War. This poem, "I'M USED TO IT," and "BENITO MUSSO-LINI," all deal with the Japanese American internment camps. In 1942, some 110,000 Japanese Americans, most of whom were American citizens, were forced to relocate to War Relocation Camps. The same treatment was not given to Italian Americans and German Americans.

The scholar in "FORCED MARCH" draws some of his imagery from classical Chinese poems about war written by Lu You, Li Bai and Yuan Haowen. This poem, along with "REVENANT" and "FACING NANJING," are set during the Rape of Nanjing. After the Japanese army occupied the Chinese city of Nanjing on December 9, 1937, they set out on a six-week campaign of brutality in which they massacred several hundred thousand civilians and raped tens of thousands of women.

Although "HOSPITAL TENT" is based upon Walt Whitman's Civil War Poem "A March in the Ranks Hard-prest, and the Road Un-known," it draws its imagery of the Philippines, gangrene and surgery, from the oral history of Capt. Ann Bernatitus, NC, USN, (Ret.), posted online by the Department of the Navy–Naval Historical Center at http//www.history.navy.mil/faqs/faq87-3b.htm

"THE BATAAN DEATH MARCH." In 1942, after the Japanese captured the Philippine island of Bataan, American and Filipino prisoners of war were marched 60 miles to prison camps. The Japanese soldiers brutalized the prisoners, deprived them of food and water, marched them to exhaustion, and casually killed thousands of them. More than a fourth of the 75,000 diseased, starved, and dehydrated prisoners died en route.

"RHINESTONES AND COLOGNE" is based in part on prisoner accounts of concerts and minstrel shows in the POW camps, but more directly was written as a "bouts-rimés poem" in which one person makes a list of rhymed words and gives it to another person who writes a poem ending in those rhymes in the same order. The bouts-rimés rhymes were developed for the literary magazine *Court Green* in 2005.

"CAMP MORALE" is based on the chapter "Morale" in Robert S. La Forte, Ronald E. Marcello, Richard L. Himmel, *With Only the Will to Live: Accounts of Americans in Japanese Prison Camps, 1941-1945.* I found this chapter very moving, particularly how so many of the men interviewed spoke of the strange phenomenon of prisoners simply giving up hope, shutting in on themselves, and dying in short order. Most of the prisoners interviewed were at camps other than Corregidor, but I use the one camp here to stand in for the many.

"BERIBERI" draws from many accounts of horrific disease among POW's and soldiers (jungle rot, beriberi, and dysentery), but is especially inspired by the language and details of Anton Bilek's oral history in Studs Terkel's *The Good War.*

"REVERSAL AT THE BATTLE OF MIDWAY" is based upon an oral history by Mitsuo Fuchida, posted online at http://www.eyewitnesstohistory.com/midway.htm. The Japanese aircraft carrier Akagi participated in the attack on Pearl Harbor. She was sunk in the Battle of Midway on June 5th, 1942. In keeping with the theme of tactical reversal, the rhymes in the poem are all "reverse rhymes" (either phonetic or letter-by-letter) so that "saw" becomes "was" and "came" becomes "make." The Battle of Midway has often been considered the turning point in the Pacific campaign. It was the American navy's first major victory in the campaign, and it weakened the Japanese fleet, which lost four aircraft carriers and a heavy cruiser.

"MASSACRE BAY" and "THE ISLAND OF WOMEN" are based on my interview with Navy Crew Chief and Top Turret Gunner Gilbert Henkins, who participated in the Aleutian Islands Campaign in 1943.

"THE BATTLE FOR SAIPAN" recounts the invasion of Saipan in June of 1944, and in particular the suicide of hundreds of civilians from the "suicide cliffs" at the north end of the island. As in Okinawa, the civilian population had been convinced by Japanese propaganda that the Americans were brutal rapists and murderers and that suicide was preferable to being captured by them. Many other civilians committed suicide by gathering around grenades given them by the Japanese army. 22,000 civilians died in the invasion of Saipan. The speaker in this poem is a Japanese American soldier in the Military Intelligence Service who was attached to a combat unit in the invasion of Saipan and who worked doing interrogations of prisoners, cracking codes, infiltrating enemy lines, and translating diaries, maps and other captured documents.

"THE MAN I LEFT ALIVE" is modeled after "Sniper," by Bernard Gutteridge, which begins:

> Moves in the rocks with inching fingers.
> We among the feathery banana trees
> Imagine for him his aim: the steel helmet
> And English face filling the backsight's V.

See also Thomas Hardy's poem, "The Man He Killed."

"THE DROWNED MAN" is a reimagining of Ariel's lovely song in Shakespeare's *The Tempest*:

> Full fathom five thy father lies;
> Of his bones are coral made;
> Those are pearls that were his eyes;
> Nothing of him does fade,
> But doth suffer a sea-change
> Into something rich and strange.
> Sea-nymphs hourly ring his knell:
> Ding-dong.
> Hark! Now hear them—Ding-dong, bell.

The story itself comes from an oral history by Vice Admiral Lawson P. Ramage, in *The Pacific War Remembered*, by John T. Mason, Jr. Ramage commanded the sub that sank a picket ship, after which "we closed in and saw about five survivors in the water. We were trying to see if we could pick up any of them, though not with any great enthusiasm because we were still on our way out to our patrol area. But none of the people in the water showed any inclination to come on board. As a matter of fact, they swam away from us. We had initially counted five, but then all of a sudden we were missing one. To our great surprise we found that one fellow had pulled a bucket over his head and was looking out through it, trying to keep from being seen and picked up. There was nothing more we could do there, so we continued on our way." I was interested in this peculiar story, and wondered what was going through the mind of the man with the bucket.

"BEACH LANDING, IWO JIMA," "GRACE UNDER PRESSURE," "SEEDS OF GOLD," "BANZAI CHARGE," and "THE CAVE" are set during the invasion of the island of Iwo Jima in February to March of 1945. The island was very powerfully fortified, with vast bunkers, and a complex of tunnels, snipers, and pillboxes, and it was fiercely defended by 22,000 Japanese soldiers, virtually all of whom fought to the death. Of the American soldiers who participated in the attack, one in three were killed or wounded.

"SEEDS OF GOLD" is based partly on a passage in Charles Kundert's oral history in *Into the Rising Sun*, in which he talks about "two buddies from Kentucky. These two were knocking gold out of the Japanese and all that kind of stupidity. When things got tough, you couldn't find them. When the shooting really got heavy or the mortars got heavy all of a sudden, they were sick, complaining of stomachaches. But when it came time to collect gold teeth, they were great. I used to call them 'mouth-fighters': talk a great war but when the shooting starts, you can't find them." Similar episodes are spoken of in *The Good War* and *Carrier Warfare in the Pacific*, among other places, detailing how (as in Joseph Heller's World War II novel, *Catch-22*) a certain number of men used the war to get rich through procurement and "harvesting."

"HERO" and "YELLOWBELLY" are based on various oral histories in Studs Terkel's *The Good War*, sometimes quite elliptically ("Yellowbelly," for example, riffs off of a brief passage in a fascinating interview with a conscientious objector in that volume in which the C.O. mentions being on a train with Native Americans who refused "to fight the white man's war," though the poem also blends in details from other C.O. oral histories).

"THE CANNIBALS" and "WHITE PIG, DARK PIG" are based upon transcripts, oral testimonies, reports and memoirs about cannibalism in New Guinea and the Philippines in Yuki Tanaka's *Hidden Horrors: Japanese War Crimes in World War II*, and on oral histories in *Into the Rising Sun*, *Senso*, and *The Good War*.

"THE CANNIBALS" is a bouts-rimés poem based on the rhyme words of Edna St. Vincent Millay's sonnet "If I should learn in some quite casual way."

"STRANGE VIGIL ON THE FIELD ONE NIGHT," "THE DEAD," "MASS SUICIDE, OKINAWA," "WHITE FEAR," and "THE DOLL" are set during the extraordinarily bloody American invasion of the island of Okinawa, during which over 100,000 Japanese troops were killed, and more than 50,000 Allied troops and hundreds of thousands of civilians suffered casualties or were killed.

"MASS SUICIDE, OKINAWA," is based on various accounts, but draws key images from Kinjo Shigeaki's oral history in *Japan at War*. During the invasion of Okinawa there were civilian casualties in the hundreds of thousands. Many were killed, and many more committed suicide. Okinawan civilians were used as human shields by the Japanese army, many Okinawan women were raped, and, worse, many killed themselves because they had been convinced by Japanese propaganda that the Americans were monsters who would kill, rape, and brutalize them if they were captured.

"THE DOLL" treats the massive use of kamikaze attacks (1900 of them) during the battle for Okinawa.

"STRANGE VIGIL ON THE FIELD ONE NIGHT" is based on Walt Whitman's Civil War poem "Vigil Strange I Kept on the Field One Night" and on a number of oral histories about the battle for Okinawa.

"THE DEATH OF PRIVATE K" is based on the testimony of witnesses, in letters to the editor of *Asahi Shimbun*, titled "Stabbing a Wounded Friend" and "Ghosts of Soldiers Lost on Guadalcanal," about the plight of Japanese soldiers in retreat in the Philippines. The letters are reprinted in *Senso: The Japanese Remember the Pacific War.*

"THE BALL TURRET GUNNER" is a reimagining of the experience of the ball turret gunner. Small men were chosen to hang from the bottom of a B-17 Flying Fortress inside a cramped rotating plexiglass ball and shoot at incoming planes with two fifty caliber machine guns. See also Randall Jarrell's poem, "The Death of the Ball Turret Gunner."

"THE UNDERWATER SHIP" and "THE SHAPE OF FEAR" are set during the disastrous sinking of the U.S.S. Indianapolis, a U.S. Navy cruiser that was attacked in the Philippine Sea by a Japanese submarine on July 26, 1945 and that sank rapidly, in just twelve minutes, with a loss of 300 men. The remaining 900 crewmen were left floating with little food and water, while suffering vicious shark attacks. When rescue finally came four days later, only 316 men survived.

"Gunner's Perspective" and "Fireflies over Tokyo" are set during the firebombing of Tokyo on February 24-25, 1945, during which high explosive bombs were used to shatter buildings into kindling which was then set on fire with napalm, causing a firestorm that killed 100,000 people and destroyed 16 square miles of the city.

"The Pilot's Tale" is based upon a conversation at a dinner I had with Brigadier General Paul Tibbets, the pilot of the Enola Gay, in 1995, and upon his subsequent comments at a public lecture at Whittier College. In an interview with Studs Terkel in 2002, he continued to have no regrets:

> ST: One last thing, when you hear people say, "Let's nuke 'em," "Let's nuke these people," what do you think?
>
> PT: Oh, I wouldn't hesitate if I had the choice. I'd wipe 'em out. You're gonna kill innocent people at the same time, but we've never fought a damn war anywhere in the world where they didn't kill innocent people. If the newspapers would just cut out the shit: "You've killed so many civilians." That's their tough luck for being there. (http://www.guardian.co.uk/g2/story/0,3604,769634,00.html)

"Morning in Hiroshima" and the poems that follow detail the experiences of civilian survivors of the atomic bomb blast in Hiroshima, and largely draw from Yoichi Fukushima's *Children of Hiroshima* and Michihiko Hachiya's, *Hiroshima Diary*, though many other sources were consulted.

"Milk Run" is based loosely upon various oral histories with American prisoners of war in Japanese prison camps, but much of the idiomatic expression draws from an oral history with Karnig Thomasian, Army Air Corps, prisoner of war of the Japanese in Rangoon, Burma. (http://www.tankbooks.com/interviews/karnig3.htm.)

"THE PIT" was largely inspired by "Prisoner of War Camp #1, Fukuoka, Japan, An Insight into Life and Death at a POW Camp in War-time Japan" by Wes Injerd (located at http://home.comcast. net/~winjerd/POWCamp1.htm.) This excellent website hosts many original documents, interrogations with prison guards and prisoners, photographs, and other resources about the Fukuoka firebombing and the beheading and vivisection war crimes.

"WARTIME MEDICINE" draws from "Japan admits dissecting WWII POWs" by Thomas Easton, *The Baltimore Sun* (http://www.centurychina.com/wiihist/germwar/uspow.htm#ww), also posted at http://home.comcast.net/~winjerd/Page05. htm, with other documentation. Compared to the live medical experiments of Dr. Josef Mengele in Auschwitz-Birkenau, similar experiments by WWII Japanese doctors are less known in the West. During WWII, Unit 731, a Japanese Army unit based in Manchuria, performed gruesome medical experiments on prisoners, killing thousands of captured Chinese and Russians. "Wartime Medicine" is about similar experiments that took place at Kyushu University, in Japan, where eight captured American pilots died after being dissected alive by Japanese doctors.

"NONCONFORMIST" was inspired by oral histories with a number of women who spoke of the scarceness of sugar, the aluminum and tire drives, the rationing, the neighborhood wardens who would enforce blackouts and the volunteers who'd watch in town hall towers for enemy airplanes. I was particularly interested by a moment in an interview with Esther Phelps: "Every little street, every village had a . . . warden. My husband was one. Whenever there was a blackout you had to go through the village and see that everybody's curtains were pulled, shades were pulled and that the lights were put out as much as could be. And I know that there was one family in town, not that they disagreed with the war but they said that they weren't going to shut their lights off. Nothing doing." "Nonconformist" is an attempt at imagining the perspective of the sort of irascible, independent person who would see all this as nonsense and refuse to cooperate.

"THE PERFECT LIFE" and "THE FACTORY" are about the kidnapping and sexual slavery of 200,000 or more women from across Asia, who were forced into prostitution to serve the Japanese army. These "comfort women" were beaten horrifically, starved, and raped both day and night, and in the end only around 25 percent of them survived. The Japanese government has yet to acknowledge and apologize for this war crime.

"THE POWER OF A GOD" is after Horace, Ode I.34.

"WAR GAMES" and "THE MAN WHO WON THE WAR" are based on my interviews with Dr. Caroline Heldman, a professor of political science at Occidental College.

Tony Barnstone is The Albert Upton Professor of English Language and Literature at Whittier College and has a master's in English and creative writing and Ph.D. in English literature from the University of California at Berkeley. His other books of poetry include *The Golem of Los Angeles* (Red Hen Press, 2008), which won the Benjamin Saltman Award in Poetry, *Sad Jazz: Sonnets* (Sheep Meadow Press, 2005) and *Impure* (University Press of Florida, 1998), in addition to a chapbook of poems, *Naked Magic* (Main Street Rag). He is also a distinguished translator of Chinese poetry and literary prose and an editor of literary textbooks. His books in these areas include *Chinese Erotic Poetry* (Everyman, 2007); *The Anchor Book of Chinese Poetry* (Anchor, 2005); *Out of the Howling Storm: The New Chinese Poetry* (Wesleyan, 1993); *Laughing Lost in the Mountains: Poems of Wang Wei* (University Press of New England, 1991); *The Art of Writing: Teachings of the Chinese Masters* (Shambhala, 1996); and the textbooks *Literatures of Asia, Africa and Latin America, Literatures of Asia,* and *Literatures of the Middle East* (all from Prentice Hall). Among his awards are the Grand Prize of the Strokestown International Poetry Festival and a Pushcart Prize in poetry, as well as fellowships from the National Endowment for the Arts and the California Arts Council. Born in Middletown, Connecticut, and raised in Bloomington, Indiana, Barnstone has lived in Greece, Spain, Kenya, and China.